The Secret Language of Women

by Sherrie Weaver

Great Quotations
Publishing Company
Glendale Heights,
Illinois

0 43422 69543 0

Cover Illustration by Design Dynamics, Glen Ellyn, IL

Published by Great Quotations Publishing Co.,
Glendale Heights, IL

ISBN 1-56245-224-X

Printed in Hong Kong

Table of Contents

If You Really Loved Me,
You'd Know What I Mean....

In **The Secret Language of Men**, we came down
pretty hard on the guys. Let's face it, as women we
have the same type of subtle nuances in our speech
that men do. It's just that we won't let the guys
make fun of us. So, as a lifelong woman, a wife and
mother, and a moderately successful cook, I offer
this little collection to the men - for their enjoyment,
and a decided edge in their next inter-gender
argument. Sorry, ladies, but we have to be fair.

CHAPTER ONE

Relationships and Other Bad Ideas

When she says: "You're so sweet to me."

She means: "I want you to go make me a sandwich."

When she says: "I love you."

She means: "You can park your truck in my driveway."

When she says: "The receptionist got engaged today, and you should see the ring her fiance gave her."

She means: "Mine isn't nearly big enough."

When she says: 'Do you think she's pretty?'

She means: "Deny it, or face a really unpleasant weekend."

When she says: "Whatever you want is fine, honey."

She means: "You are doomed. Whatever you choose will be wrong."

When she says: "I don't want to talk about it."

She means: "You had better ask me what's wrong about 50 more times."

When she says: "I think I'm falling in love with you."

She means: "I'm beginning to think I could tolerate you for some period of time."

When she says: "If you really loved me, you'd know what I mean."

She means: "I have no idea why I'm upset, I just know it's your fault."

When she says: "Will you always love me?"

She means: "I've just driven your truck into an irrigation ditch."

When she says: "Can't we just cuddle up?"

She means: "The electric blanket isn't working."

When she says: "Isn't this romantic?"

She means: "It is, and you'd better be, REAL soon."

When she says: "Is that your old girlfriend?"

She means: "Now is the time for you to begin telling me how much better I am for you."

When she says: "I ran into my old boyfriend today."

She means: "You are now in for two full days of hearing how well he's doing and how fine he treated me."

When she says: "We need to re-evaluate our relationship."

She means: "It's a wedding ring or the road, buddy."

When she says: "Do you know what day today is?"

She means: "You have forgotten an event of great importance, and are going to pay dearly for it."

When she says: "You're not the only fish in the sea, you know."

She means: "It may be time for me to drop the bait into the waves and see if anything nibbles."

When she says: "I told you so."

She means: "Any idea you have will meet with merciless ridicule."

When she says: "You never send me flowers anymore."

She means: "We have officially been together long enough to have a pretty serious argument."

When she says: "You're late."

She means: "You are in for a questioning session that will make the Spanish Inquisition seem tame."

When she says: "You just don't understand."

She means: "And I don't have the slightest intention of explaining."

When she says: "You are a part of me."

She means: "I have begun to figure your income into my budget."

When she says: "I have a headache."

She means: "Don't even think about it."

When she says: "There was one of those 'Are You Compatible?' quizzes in my woman's magazine."

She means: "We aren't."

When she says: "I do."

She means: "And he will."

When she says: "Nobody's perfect."

She means: "Except the guy I dated right before I met you."

When she says: "I've had enough of you."

She means: "Nothing you can say or do will get you out of this."

When she says: "But that's different....."

She means: "You have come dangerously close to applying logic and equality to this argument, and you know that is not allowed."

When she says: "You've changed so much lately."

She means: *"Explain yourself."*

When she says: "Jealous? Of course I'm not jealous."

She means: "You will be under intense surveillance for the rest of your natural life."

When she says: "What would you do without me?"

She means: "The only answer that will ensure you will see tomorrow is, 'I don't know'."

When she says: "I just don't see your point."

She means: "Selective perception is a wonderful thing."

When she says: "No, I don't blame you."

She means: "At least not to your face."

When she says: "Well, I do want to talk about it."

She means: *"So hang on, because here we go."*

When she says: "You drive me crazy."

She means: "I can't figure you out, and that annoys me."

When she says: "Now just let me tell you something."

She means: "Try to stop me, I dare you."

When she says: "I mean it this time."

She means: "But I didn't mean it the other sixteen times I said it."

When she says: "What are you thinking about?"

She means: "The only correct answer is 'you, honey'."

When she says: "I was worried about you."

She means: "I was afraid you were getting away with something."

When she says: "Why are you so grouchy?"

She means: "That's MY job."

When she says: "You men all want one thing, and one thing only."

She means: "Another nap?"

When she says: "You don't love me anymore."

She means: "You didn't hug me when you came home from work today."

When she says: "You could have called to tell me you were going to be late."

She means: *"Unless you were pinned in the wreckage of a gruesome car accident, you will be sleeping on the sofa tonight."*

When she says: "The secret to a good marriage is communication."

She means: "Sit down and listen."

When she says: "I thought you said she was just an old friend."

She means: "I have been through your yearbook and discovered several incriminating messages that you will spend the next three days trying to deny."

When she says: "I can't believe you forgot our anniversary."

She means: *"You will regret this for the rest of your life. In fact, I'm thinking of having it engraved on your tombstone."*

When she says: "Go away and leave me alone."

She means: "Come here and hold me."

CHAPTER TWO

Money and Other Legends

When she says: "It doesn't take a lot of money to make me happy."

She means: "Just whatever you've got will do nicely."

When she says: "We never do anything fun anymore."

She means: "Take me out and spend money on me."

48

When she says: "You never make me feel attractive anymore."

She means: "It's time for a new outfit, a fancy dinner and expensive wine."

When she says: "My best friend's husband just got a big raise."

She means: "You need to bring home more money."

When she says: "A man your age should know better."

She means: "Cut the ponytail, and don't even think about buying that sports car."

When she says: "I am so tired of thinking up new ideas for dinner."

She means: "PLEASE take me out to eat."

When she says: "I don't have anything to wear."

She means: "I'm headed to the mall with your plastic."

53

When she says: "Do you get paid today?"

She means: "I've written a $500 check to the shoe store and can't cover it."

54

When she says: "I'm craving French food."

She means: "Guess which expensive restaurant we'll be visiting tonight?"

When she says: "I got you some new shirts today."

She means: "To distract you from the entire new wardrobe I bought myself."

When she says: "It's cold in here."

She means: "Turn the heat up to 82°, and I don't want to hear the words 'power bill'."

When she says: "I just need a little time alone."

She means: "I'm going to the mall."

When she says: "I think we're in a rut."

She means: "We need new furniture, new carpeting and new drapes."

59

When she says: "I know money doesn't grow on trees."

She means: "But I keep hoping."

When she says: "Let's just call out for pizza tonight."

She means: "We have nothing in the kitchen but two cans of stewed prunes."

61

When she says: "I have an idea."

She means: "This is going to be time-consuming, expensive and probably painful."

When she says: "Winter is coming."

She means: "I want a new coat, boots and gloves."

63

When she says: "Oh, look at that bracelet."

She means: "Buy it for me, without hesitation."

64

When she says: "Honey, do you have a couple of dollars?"

She means: "Because I sure don't."

65

When she says: "We just need a couple of things."

She means: "Get a cart and prepare to shop."

When she says: "Let's celebrate your promotion."

She means: "Did you get enough of a raise to afford a really fancy dinner?"

67

When she says: "I found the best bargain today."

She means: "And made up for it by shopping twice as long."

68

CHAPTER THREE

Family, The Ties that Knot Up

When she says: "I think it's time we settled down."

She means: "I'm pregnant."

When she says: "Have you ever thought about having children?"

She means: "I forgot to take my birth control pill."

When she says: "No, I like your mother just fine."

She means: "From a very great distance."

When she says: "Your kids are driving me completely over the edge."

She means: "Take them for a drive so that I can watch TV without being interrupted."

When she says: "I talked to my mother today."

She means: "Clean out the guest room, and prepare to have your life turned upside down."

When she says: "My mother was right about you."

She means: *"And I will never let you forget it."*

When she says: "He's your son."

She means: "He really screwed up this time."

When she says: "This house is too small."

She means: "My brother and his four kids are moving in."

When she says: "Of course I like your Aunt Edna."

She means: "She's old, sick, rich and you're her favorite nephew."

When she says: "Your son is sick."

She means: "You will be taking the day off work to tend to him."

When she says: "Your mother called today."

She means: "The subject of this evening's argument will be your family."

When she says: "I have got to go on a diet."

She means: "You had better disagree with me real quick, or it's going to be a long, cold weekend."

CHAPTER FOUR

Recreation and Beer, a Redundancy?

When she says: "I think we're compatible."

She means: "You have a boat, and I like to water-ski."

When she says: "A little culture won't hurt you one bit."

She means: "I have tickets to the ballet, and if you doze off, I will hurt you."

When she says: "We had the kids when we were so young, we never really got a chance to walk on the wild side."

She means: "We are going to take Country Swing lessons, and yes, you have to wear that silly hat."

83

When she says: "That nasty, smelly dog of yours has got to go."

She means: "I bought a cat."

84

When she says: "Why don't you go play basketball with your buddies?"

She means: "Several of my friends are coming over this afternoon, and we want to ridicule you unmercifully."

85

When she says: "You rented another Western movie?"

She means: "You should have rented an insipid romance movie, where the hero is everything you will never be, and I can tell you that all afternoon."

When she says: "I'm almost ready."

She means: "Pull up a chair, buddy, we aren't going anywhere for hours."

87

When she says: "Is that what you're wearing?"

She means: "Go change your clothes."

When she says: "I need a vacation."

She means: "Take me to a place where there is a beach, an open bar and room service."

89

When she says: "Why don't you watch the ball game today?"

She means: "I'm up to something, and don't want you to catch me until it's too late for you to stop me."

When she says: "I'm going out with the girls tonight."

She means: "We are going to drink white wine spritzers and talk about the men we know, while you stay home, watch TV, and enjoy a couple of hours of peace."

91

When she says: "There's a great movie on TV tonight."

She means: "Get ready to sit through 'THE KING AND I' for the 100th time."

When she says: "I just love Sundays alone with you."

She means: "Reach for those golf clubs and you're a dead man."

93

When she says: "Let's go do something before we waste the whole day."

She means: "I am afraid that you have taken root on that sofa."

94

When she says: "I've got to make a couple of phone calls."

She means: "You won't see or hear from me again for several hours."

95

When she says: "I don't care, watch what you want."

She means: "I want to watch you throw your thumb out pushing the buttons on the remote."

When she says: "Sure, honey, I'd love to go to the sportsman's show with you."

She means: "That way I can hold on to the checkbook and credit cards."

When she says: "You always know how to make me laugh."

She means: "There is a fine line between ridicule and humor."

When she says: "We never talk anymore."

She means: "Turn off the TV."

99

When she says: "You've been drinking, haven't you?"

She means: "Why wasn't I invited?"

When she says: "I like this song."

She means: "Don't even think about changing the radio station."

101

When she says: "Oh, we just talked girl talk, honey."

She means: "My friends and I have just spent the last three hours berating and belittling our men behind your backs."

When she says: "We need a vacation."

She means: "I've just bought an entire new summer wardrobe, and I need a place to wear it."

103

When she says: "You need to stop acting like a little boy."

She means: "I just threw away your entire baseball card collection."

When she says: "Who was the woman you were dancing with when I walked in?"

She means: "If she wasn't an immediate family member, you are a walking corpse."

When she says: "Don't be silly: of course that movie didn't scare me."

She means: "I'm sleeping with the light on to discourage burglars."

When she says: "I'm tired and I want to go home now."

She means: *"That blond you've been talking to is beginning to look interested."*

107

When she says: "I'll just be a minute."

She means: "You stand a good chance of dying of old age before you see me again."

When she says: "I didn't confirm anything, honey, I merely mentioned that we might stop by."

She means: "I've rented you a tux, so clear your schedule."

When she says: "Are you ready to go?"

She means: "I am."

When she says: "Honey, the auto show will be so crowded...."

She means: "I've got tickets to the art museum."

When she says: "You know, I've never
been to Paris."

She means: "And that's your fault."

When she says: "It's a boys night out, huh?"

She means: "You will regret it intensely, so make sure you have a really good time while you can."

113 ♀

When she says: "Wouldn't you like to stop for a drink?"

She means: "I have to go to the bathroom."

114

When she says: "You're going fishing again?"

She means: "Hasn't that poor worm suffered enough?"

When she says: "You act so differently when you're around your friends."

She means: "Natural, more relaxed and a trace of sarcasm creeps into your voice when you say 'Yes, dear.'."

When she says: "It doesn't matter where we go for dinner."

She means: "As long as it doesn't have a drive-thru window."

When she says: "You mean there are ball games on all day?"

She means: "It could be a very long, gruesome day for both of us."

When she says: "Well, are the other guys taking their wives?"

She means: "Because if they are, so are you."

When she says: "No, you pick the movie."

She means: *"That way I can criticize your decision."*

120

When she says: "Remember when we used to go out on Saturday nights?"

She means: "Rent another video this weekend, and I'll hurt you."

When she says: "I'd like to go to the ball game with you."

She means: "That ought to put a damper on any fun you planned to have."

When she says: "Why don't we have lunch together?"

She means: "It has occurred to me that you may be having way too much fun at work."

When she says: "Do you like my hair this way?"

She means: "Can you tell the difference between the way it is now, and the way I usually wear it?"

CHAPTER FIVE

Work is a Four Letter Word

When she says: "I tried to call you today, but your secretary said you were out."

She means: "Where were you, what were you doing, and who were you doing it with?"

When she says: "You're working late again?"

She means: "Oh, good, something else to yell at you about."

When she says: "Boy, we sure have a lot of junk around here."

She means: "Clean the garage."

When she says: "I am getting real tired of being the house servant around here."

She means: "You left your socks on the sofa again."

When she says: "I work, too, you know."

She means: *"You fold the laundry, I don't want to."*

When she says: "There is more to life than televised sports, you know."

She means: "Take out the trash."

When she says: "I sort of resent you for the demands you make on my time."

She means: "I don't want to clean the oven."

When she says: "My car is making a funny noise."

She means: "You are going to spend the next 6 1/2 hours on the garage floor trying to figure out what could possibly be going 'chunka chunka'."

When she says: "Honey, you're such a big, strong guy."

She means: "The lid is stuck on this jelly jar."

When she says: "It's time you started helping out around the house."

She means: "I put aquarium gravel in the garbage disposal again, and it is completely locked up."

When she says: "Will you get your nasty, dirty clothes out of the bathroom?"

She means: "So I can hang up my wet nylons on the shower bar."

When she says: "Honey, what does that little red light on the car dashboard mean?"

She means: "Could it have anything to do with the fact that the engine is shooting out flames?"

When she says: "I had a really rotten day at work."

She means: "I got yelled at for gossiping with the receptionist."

When she says: "You are such a slob."

She means: "Re-fold and stack the newspaper when you're done reading it."

When she says: "It's starting to rain."

She means: "I left the windows in the car rolled down."

When she says: "I'm coming down with a bug."

She means: "You will be cooking your own dinner tonight."

When she says: "Do you like my cooking?"

She means: "Even if you are choking back waves of nausea, you had better respond in the affirmative."

When she says: "Shouldn't we just call a plumber?"

She means: "There are still bloodstains in the carpet from the last time you tried to fix something."

When she says: "I must have pulled a muscle helping you with the yardwork."

She means: "I want a backrub."

When she says: "The neighbors are having their house painted."

She means: *"Prepare to argue over a long, expensive list of home improvements."*

When she says: "Honey, will you put gas in my car?"

She means: "I don't think there is enough in the tank to make it to the station, and I don't want to be the one to walk for it."

When she says: "Are you going to be around the house today?"

She means: "I want to re-arrange the living room furniture, and I want you to do all the lifting, moving and dragging."

When she says: "We've had so much rain this spring."

She means: "Time to mow the lawn."

When she says: "It's a beautiful day."

She means: "We should do yard work."

When she says: "The radio says we'll have 13 more inches of snow by morning."

She means: "You'll have to shovel the walk twice."

When she says: "I'm trying a new recipe for dinner."

She means: "Be prepared to have your stomach pumped."

When she says: "Oh, honey, I'm sorry you don't feel well. What can I do?"

She means: "Prepare to be smothered in misguided mothering affection."

When she says: "Your steaks are always perfect."

She means: "I don't want to cook."

When she says: "I need you."

She means: "Otherwise, I'd have to change my own oil."

When she says: "You're supposed to treat me like a lady."

She means: *"You carry the heavy stuff."*

When she says: "Didn't you tell me you wanted to start lifting weights?"

She means: "I need something from the attic, and I'm sure it's buried behind a lot of boxes."

When she says: "Do you want me to fix you some breakfast?"

She means: "I'm going to hit you up for something big, and I want you to be in a good mood."

When she says: "What did you do to this place? I cleaned it before I left."

She means: "You have turned this house into your first apartment."

When she says: "EEEEEEEEK! Honey, come here, quick."

She means: "There is a spider in the bathtub, and I am ready to take a shower."

When she says: "Did you work out today?"

She means: "You smell funny."

When she says: "Can you fix it?"

She means: "Or should I call a qualified, but expensive professional?"

When she says: "I thought you let the dog out."

She means: "We are going to need extensive carpet cleaning."

When she says: "Was that your new receptionist who answered the phone when I called your office today?"

She means: "Unless she's old, ugly and married, you will be grilled on a daily basis."

When she says: "Am I getting fat?"

She means: "God, I love watching you squirm as you try to think of a good way to answer this question."

163

When she says:"I think he's such a
stud muffin...."

She means: "He has hair."